The Wonder

of

Two Lives - Two Lives

∀

Jo Ann Jones Watson

Co-authored by Minister Ernest Watson

M.O.R.E. Publishers
St. Louis, MO

The Wonder
of
Two Lives - Two Lives

∀

Jo Ann Jones Watson
Co-authored by Minister Ernest Watson

M.O.R.E. Publishers
11681 Larimore Road
Spanish Lake, MO 63138

www.MOREPublishers.biz
http://TheScaleMagazine.com
http://www.cafepress.com/MOREPublishers

The Wonder
of
Two Lives - Two Lives

$\forall$

Jo Ann Jones Watson
Co-authored by Minister Ernest Watson

Table of Contents

My Appreciation

I give my sincere gratitude to my Father in heaven. Thank you for giving me this gift of sharing my testimony to the whole world. I thank my Lord Jesus for giving me a second chance on life. I thank my Lord Jesus for his guidance in helping me write this book.

I give my deepest appreciation to my husband Rev. Ernest L. Watson for being my best friend, for taking time out of his busy schedule to help me and for giving me support when times got hard.

I also give my appreciation to my mother Fannie Jones for sharing some of the details.

I also give thanks to Angelee Coleman Grider for helping with editing and publishing my book. I also give my thanks to Akila Bryant who helped me in the initial editing of this project. I would like to give thanks to my cousin Ira Jones for his artistic work on my cover.

I would also like to make this statement: We would be negligent as Christians if we didn't pass our testimony on to the next generation. I would like for everyone to see that my Lord Jesus is still healing and blessing as He was in the Biblical times. I give all my thanks to my Lord Jesus Christ.

Now, this is my testimony.

The Biography of an Author

Jo Ann Jones Watson was born in Marshall County, Mississippi May 7, 1955, and was delivered by a midwife. She was born in an old gray frame house with a tin roof. The house had no running water or inside toilet. This house was however where true love, Jo Ann and her Grandparents lived.

Professionally, her Grandfather was a sharecropper. He worked in the fields for the white man in order to secure his living. He planted cotton. During the year, his family helped him to chop and to pick the crop in exchange for the family's rent that was paid mostly after the harvest in autumn.

Jo Ann's mother was a very active 19 year old young lady. She too was the object of a non-caring, psychologically controlling man. She had sex at a young age because she thought she was in *love. She got pregnant. He left. He was selfish, controlling, and played the game of "love them and leave them." This created problems for Jo Ann's mom and the unborn child.*

Already, in those times during the 1950's, black children weren't allowed to go to school on a regular basis. Most of school time was only six months out of a year, November- April. Then last week of September began cotton-picking time. So Jo Ann's mother wasn't able to receive the proper education for a teenager, which was complicated by pregnancy.

So, after Jo Ann was born, the Grandparents decided to send Jo Ann's mother to Memphis, Tennessee to live with her uncle. They reasoned that it was to better educate their daughter. Through obedience, Jo Ann's mother attended school as her parents wanted. The grandbaby remained in Mississippi.

In reality Jo Ann's mother knew that her parents couldn't afford to support the granddaughter that was now born. While in Memphis, the mother would need a job. So, after school she did work as a short-order cook in a small restaurant. The wages were very low, but it would help her parents to support the daughter. Then, Jo Ann's mother would go to Mississippi on the weekends to give her parents money to help wherever it was needed.

While Jo Ann was growing up she was taught the life style of Blacks in Mississippi. She learned how to pick and chop cotton. Her Grandfather gave her a small hoe that he made just for her. He instructed her on what to do. At first there was a lot of cotton chopped down until Jo Ann got into the rhythm and method of chopping. Jo

Ann's Grandfather was a very strong-willed man and he knew that it would take education and work for Jo Ann to survive in this world. In his mind he was teaching Jo Ann how to make a living.

Later when Jo Ann got home from the field her Grandmother would teach her how to do a "woman's job". They would pick peas and beans. The grandmother would also show her how to make the sweet milk, churn, and turn the milk into butter milk after skimming the butter. The process would be to remove the butter from the top of the milk and put it into a butter dish. That would be served with meals or for cooking. Jo Ann really didn't know what was happening. All she understood was that she was helping the Grandparents. Most of the time it was fun.

In the mornings Jo Ann was up and out with her Grandfather. He would call her by her nickname Koody. He would say, "Come on Koody".

She would jump up and put on her little pants and boots for she was no more then 3 or 4 years old, and more of a Granddaddy's child. So she helped with the morning chores and milking cows. Jo Ann had her own special cow and of course she had her own little bucket. Her Granddaddy had even made her a little wooden stool to sit on just like his.

This process continued until Jo Ann's Grandmother expired. Jo Ann was six years old. Then it was evident that her mother had to take the child to Memphis, Tennessee to live. Her Granddaddy was unable to care for a little girl alone. Jo Ann was so sad to leave her Granddaddy alone. In her mind, she sometimes thought she was taking care of him. But Jo Ann's mother told her that they would visit her Granddaddy often. Jo Ann was very happy with that decision because she truly loved her Granddaddy. He was the type of man she wanted to marry.

∀

The Ways Of A Controlling Man

I am Tammy, and just as Tammy learned, every "princess" should understand the way some men try to maintain control over women. For example, Mother was a very active 19-year-old who became pregnant and became a single mother. The man used her youth and little experience to control her.

Then Tammy's first love was Earl, a man that was older than she. Earl knew Tammy didn't know very much. So, he played on her social intelligence. Tammy really loved Earl though. Yet, as this was evident, he figured ways he could use things to control her. Earl, being Tammy's first lover and being older, maneuvered their dating and love-making. Then Tammy got pregnant.

Surprisingly, Earl's mother found out and was devastated. Little did Tammy know, Earl was seeing another woman. But, Earl's mother and family knew.

"If there's anything I can do for you and the baby just let me know," Earl's mother did advise Tammy. Earl's mother also told Tammy not to believe everything that her son said.

"But I love Earl and he loves me," Tammy naively replied.

Finally frustration grew in Earl's mother voice. "Tammy you are young and dumb. You don't know nothing about men. You need to just slow it down and take your time."

When Earl came home from the Marines, Earl's mother knew that Earl would spend some time with another girl before he went to see Tammy. The phone started ringing constantly. Tammy was calling him to see if he was in town. Earl never answered her calls.

Tears showed her emotions. Tammy really thought that they were going to get married. Then one day he finally called. "We will have to move to another state," he insisted.

"No, I'm not ready to leave home yet," she frantically insisted. "I want to finish my career."

Surprisingly, Earl didn't push the issue. He was happy to know that Tammy wasn't going to leave her hometown.

Already confused, Tammy called Earl back in a couple of days after she became calmer. She did consider the marriage proposal and planned to move out of town. After all, she loved him.

"Why haven't you called me?" she asked.

"I went on and got married to someone else who would leave town since you didn't want to go with me," he said straightforwardly.

This was one of the signs of being controlled through love. Earl figured out the one thing that Tammy wouldn't do. That was his way of getting out of marrying her. Since being in the Marines, Earl knew that he needed an older woman and Tammy was only 17 years old. Earl was 21 and gained experience while he had been away from home in the Marines. At first, Earl wanted a woman and no attachments. Then while maturing, he wanted a woman.

"I wanted to tell you that Earl was seeing someone else," his mother said as she broke down in tears, "but you were so in love with him. This is why I was telling you not to put all your hope in Earl. I'm glad you didn't leave town with Earl. He might have gotten you somewhere and left you."

Tammy could only respond with, "Yea I understand now, but I thought you didn't like me, and I thought he loved me."

"What can I say?" she asked. "You did the right thing and everything is going to work out. You'll find a man that will love you for who you are, and not control you for what he can get."

God helped Tammy grow with wisdom. One day an unusual encounter occurred. Tammy, Earl, and his wife were at the same store. The baby was with her. Earl walked by her and the baby. He didn't look towards them. He didn't say a word. He didn't acknowledge them.

Truth hit Tammy. Earl didn't leave town. He stayed right there. He had used her, though she believed in him.

God still helped her life get better even though she did not acknowledge Him through her ordeal. Then Tammy met Bob. Unfortunately, the relationship with Bob was controlled by physical and mental abuse. Tammy refused to see the signs once more because when they first met, he was so nice. He always showered her and her son with expensive gifts.

She ignored "the little things" including the fact that she was on the rebounds. Yet Bob knew Tammy would work hard and some day she would have nice things. He could tell that Tammy had a very strong mind to succeed in whatever she put her mind to do. So Bob and Tammy later married. Then the big sign of turmoil began. One day Bob jokingly said to Tammy, "I'll kill you if you leave me."

For a long time, he never did anything to her after that statement, so she stayed. She looked at Bob though with disbelief. Yet he only returned the look with a smile. Instinctively though she knew he was serious about the statement. Because of circumstances in their lives, Bob realized he needed to control Tammy with fear for he saw the God-given maturity in her.

Yes, Tammy stayed. Nothing else drastic happened until time passed and their daughter was born. There were signs of Bob attempting to fulfill the statement that he had made to Tammy. In fact, on June 12, 1979, the Lord Jesus Christ had to save Tammy's life.

This time she was not controlled by love mentally. Bob wanted to control her with fear. It wasn't about love. He knew that he couldn't find a reason to fight or slap her around. She worked. She came home and did everything he said for her to do. Yet without revealing it, Bob also knew Tammy only married him because she was hurt by another man. He was resentful.

Because of resentment, he shot her five times. Don't miss the details coming in the rest of the story. You see, ironically, Tammy was able to pull out of the relationship, but she was near death. Still though, did she not learn her lesson of how to pick the right man? No, but God showed her the true love of Him for His daughter.

The third man, Lee, was not controlling. Lee was the type of man that was "in control" of his life. He knew what he wanted out of life. He was the type of man to take on life's situations as they occurred.

So he didn't look for women like Tammy to stand up for her family, and be the man and the woman image. He would always stand up and do the things that a man should do. Lee respected Tammy as being a wife, mother, and woman. He told Tammy to "let a man be a man".

He taught Tammy that there were things that a man had to do. Also, he explained that there were some things only a woman could do. Lee explained to Tammy that he would make decisions and they would talk things over first. This was the type of man for which Tammy was longing - just like her Granddad. This was the type of man Tammy really needed. Lee was so much different from the other men she had before.

Meeting Lee was when Tammy realized that there was a difference in "a man in control", and not "trying to control" her. He wanted the best for her and her children and them as a family. Tammy always wanted a man that would stand up for her. She didn't want one to manipulate her as the men she had in her life before she met Lee.

Time passed and Tammy and Lee grew very much in love with each other. Tammy thought this was a marriage made in heaven. Everything was going alright even though they had their ups and down. Lee and Tammy didn't always think on the same level, but they were always able to come to agreements. If there were no agreements, Lee would make the decisions, and that was okay with Tammy.

In retrospect, Tammy's experience taught her that there were three aspects of a "controlling man".

1. Love--A man knows that if you love him he can control you.

2. Fear--A man knows that if you fear him he will control you.

3. LOVE--Love is when a man is in control, but not controlling.

∞

Tammy's Teenage Love Life

I am Tammy. I was shot five times trying to get out of a poor relationship.

Before I met God I was in two abusive relationships. That also was before I met my present, loving husband who is helping me write this story today.

This story is written to inspire any female to be strong, especially if you are still in an abusive relationship. Trust God and believe that He will fix the situation for you. I am a testimony that He will.

I can testify that because of one of the abusers, I ended up paralyzed in the hospital. Then I really met God. As I lay there on the cold hospital table, unable to talk fluently with my Mom, and clinging to life the best that I knew how, God came to me in a dream. He talked to me.

I saw him sitting beside the railing on my bed. He reached out for me and pulled me up because I was falling fast into a state of death.

"Tammy, everything will be all right," He said. "You must trust me and believe in me, even though things look very dark."

"I don't know what to do," I calmly cried.

"Take my hand. Learn of me," He said.

Though frightened, I decided to trust God for the things God said to me. Before He vanished, He said, "Remember where you came from. Go back and I will renew you."

Adulthood came at a young age to me, Tammy Faye. I was 16 years old when I thought I had found the love of my life. We dated for two years and I was deeply in love with Earl.

I sensed that there were some things that I did not know about him and that there was some unusual distance between the two of us. Yet, feeling this way, I also felt that if I would have a baby by Earl, the responsibility would keep the relationship closer.

Several months later after beginning to date and have sex, the miracle happened. I became pregnant by Earl. However, after Earl found out, it seemed that even though he brought home an income, he struggled to find enough money to take care of three people. He tried to find a job but he wasn't successful. Then he decided to enlist in the Marines after he finished high school.

So, June of 1970 Earl left for South Carolina. All the time while Earl was in service he verbally said that he planned to marry when he was discharged. We constantly wrote to each other. Earl would even call when he got a chance.

Finally, Earl was able to come home to see his son when he was one week old. It seemed that the proud dad was so excited to see his son and me, his future wife. One clue was that he showed the baby off to everyone. Earl spent as much time as he could with his son and me, or so I thought. After his week was over once again we had to say goodbye. I even went to the airport with his mother, who I greatly admired. I thought she loved me. She was wonderful to me.

Continuing to write to each other, I told him every little thing the baby did; from cutting teeth to crawling. Then I noticed that things started to change.

In June 1973 Earl came home again, I thought he said he was to get discharged out of the Marines soon. He however, said that he wanted me and our son to go back to South Carolina with him.

I had just graduated from high school and had a job now working as a salesgirl down town in a department store. I was just getting a feel of responsibility. Besides, there was no way I was going to leave my Mama. As an only child, even though Tammy Faye loved Earl, she was only 18 years old and had never been out of town without her mother. When Earl supposedly, officially proposed and strangely confronted me about moving, you could say Tammy Faye panicked. I was a child in an adult situation. At this point the circumstances had changed. It wasn't just letter writing or telephone talk. It was real.

Earl was also a few years older than me. He was ready to be on his own. I thought very hard but I was just too afraid to leave the comfort zone. I told Earl that I would not be going and we could get married after he got out of the Marines for good.

Earl hung up the telephone in my face, that night. Subconsciously I thought, "He'll be all right. I'll call him tomorrow when I get off work."

However, when I got off work the next day, I called Earl. "I can't," he stuttered. "I can't talk to you because I have just gotten married."

I began to cry. "Why?" I was so shocked. "Were you dating someone else while we were together?"

"No I just met her. One of my friends introduced us."

"Oh my God," I thought. "Didn't Earl have more feelings in his heart for me?" Since it hurt so badly, I'm going to tell the story the way Tammy Faye would do it.

Tammy called Kay, one of her best friends and began to tell Kay what had happened. Then Kay turned around and began to tell Fay.

"Tammy, Girl just come over my house," Kay squealed. "Fay is over here. We need to talk to you." Tammy's mother agreed to keep the baby so the three could have a girls' evening out. Tammy broke down in tears when she arrived at Kay's door.

"Girl what are you crying for?" asked Fay who was trying to comfort her. "There's more fish in the sea."

Not to make matters any worse, but Kay said, "Girl that's why I didn't fool with him. I knew the ass hole was no good."

Tammy defended him still. "Yes, I understand but I loved him. I thought we were going to get married."

"Girl ain't you glad you didn't leave home? I knew he wasn't right," responded Kay.

"Yea you're right", Tammy said as she finally stopped crying. "I'm glad I didn't go."

The three played cards (gin) and played music to cheer up. Haphazardly, of all the songs, Kay accidentally put on "Love and Happiness".

"Take that off!" Tammy screamed.

"Yeah," Fay retorted. "Put on Brick House. We can get us a man, girl. We're brick houses."

Tammy went home after her evening out, feeling somewhat better. Then looking at her son, she said to herself, "I do know one man that loves me, I just haven't prayed to Him in a long time." She smiled, and went to bed.

The Unusual Marriage

Time passed. Suddenly, one day Tammy saw a guy at the store which was an old high school classmate. His name was Bob.

"Are you okay?" Bob asked. "I heard what happened to you. Are you okay? I'm sorry. I didn't mean to just spring that on you, but I saw Kay last week and we were talking."

"Oh it didn't work out," Tammy finally responded. "He decided to go his way and I decided to go mine."

"Give me your phone number," Bob told Tammy. "I'll call you when I get off work one evening, okay? Maybe we can go out to dinner."

"I'll give you my phone number; we can talk, but I don't know about all that going out," snapped Tammy.

"Why?" insisted Bob.

"I don't think I'm ready right now," she bowed her head and replied.

"So I guess we'll just talk," Bob said.

Tammy later called Fay and asked her did she remember a guy named Bob who went to high school with them?

"Yea I remember girl."

"Did you also know Kay told Bob about me and Earl breaking up?"

"Girl," giggled Fay, "I told you she is like a refrigerator. She can't keep nothing. Whatever goes in must come out."

"Bob asked me for my phone number, and

he said he wants to call me one day after he gets off work. He asked could he take me out to dinner." Fay, what do you think?" demanded Tammy.

"Girl I didn't know he was working. Where he working at?"

"I didn't ask him all of that," Tammy snapped. "I told him he could call me, but I didn't know about going out with him."

Fay asked and reminded Tammy, "You do know how wild he use to be in high school. Does it seem like he has changed any?"

"Seems like he is more settled now," Tammy thought for a moment. "I don't know."

"You better check him out before you go out with him. You know how he use to be."

Later Tammy confronted Kay. "Kay, why did you tell Bob about me and Earl?"

"You know he had been liking you all through high school," Kay replied. "…and he asked me about you. I told him you had just gone through a break up. Tammy, I just think you need to get out some instead of sitting around the house."

"Yea, but I just don't want you to just tell all my business…Kay I'll talk to him to see just what he's about."

Within two days, Bob called Tammy.

Tammy said, "I'm doing alright."

"You didn't think I was going to call did you?" Bob laughed.

"No, you know how you use to lie all the time."

"You remember that? But, that was the high school days. Now, I'm a man now!"

Tammy said, "Yea right !"

Bob said, "You know I've always wanted you , but you never would act right."

"What do you mean, I wouldn't act right?" Tammy snapped back.

"I tried to talk to you," Bob defended. "You wouldn't talk to me. I wanted to walk you home from school and you wouldn't walk with me. Even when I got my car you didn't want to ride with me."

"You knew I was dating Earl then."

"Yeah, and I told you that he was no good," Bob snapped.

"How did you know he wasn't no good?" asked Tammy.

"We use to hang together. Yea, he even tried to talk to Kay your best friend, while he was dating you."

"No. I don't believe that. Kay would have told me, because she knew how much I liked him."

Bob lowered his voice, "I thought you knew."

"No this is the first time I heard this," Tammy screamed.

"I'm not trying to start nothing, but I knew how tight you and Kay were."

Later Tammy called Kay. "Why didn't you tell me you and Earl were trying to get together while he was still dating me?"

Stunned, Kay said, "I thought you knew Earl liked me?"

Tammy said, "How am I s'pose to know?"

"Remember when Earl would drop us off from school? I was on his way home. I would be the last one to be dropped off. That's when he would try to talk to me."

Tammy said, "Why didn't you tell me?"

"I told Earl you and I were friends, and I couldn't do you like that. I just left it at that. I didn't think about it any more."

"You should have told me."

"If I had told you what would you have done?"

"If you had told me, I might have believed that he didn't love me, and I might not have gotten pregnant."

"Don't put that on me," Kay snapped. "You got pregnant because you were trying to keep him."

"Yea but I thought he loved me and we were going to get married.

"I'm sorry," Kay replied. "If I had of known you thought you were going to get married, I would have told you. Somehow though, I thought he loved you too."

When Tammy's mom, Mae came home, she looked at Tammy and knew something was wrong. She didn't say anything though. She stood at Tammy's door, just smiling.

"I'm off work tomorrow," Tammy finally said. "If you come home early I'd like to talk to you Mom."

"Okay I'll be looking forward to talking to you too; seems like something is bothering you."

"Yea I just need to talk Mom."

Tammy went on to work that evening deeply thinking of some of the things that had happened in her life with Earl. She thought of the things that Kay had said. Also she thought of what she just found out about her best friend and her boy friend. What would have been the right thing to do, Tammy wondered.

Mae went to work and returned early that next evening. She called Tammy into the kitchen where all their family discussions were done. Tammy nervously took a seat at the table.

"Mom I found out some things that I didn't

know and I wonder that if I had found out any earlier would the information have made a difference?"

Mae asked, "What was it you found out baby?"

"Mom my best friend Kay knew something unsettling about my boyfriend, and she didn't tell me. She said nothing happened." Tammy went on to explain the situation about Earl to her mom.

"Baby let me tell you this, when you tell a woman something about that man that she's in love with, most women won't believe it. They will think that their girlfriend wants that man and you can lose friendship when you talk to that woman about that man. And if nothing happened it's best that some things are left alone."

"But we were friends!"

"It doesn't matter," explained Mae. "When a woman is in love, she thinks the whole world is against that love. She will reason that others are just jealous."

"Mom maybe you're right. On second thought if Kay had told me I might not have believed her. Earl had my nose too far opened for me to believe anything about him."

"This is what I'm saying. You are good friends. You don't want to lose the friendship if nothing didn't happen."

"Thanks Mom, that's what I needed to hear."

"Oh yea, by the way Bob called and what's going on with that?"

"Mom, Bob had called the other day and asked if we could get together and go out."

"I don't know, you still know how much trouble he used to get into when you all were in high school?"

Tammy said, "Yea Mom he said he has changed."

"Well honey, the only advice I got for you is to be careful, take it easy, and to take it slow. Don't rush into anything like you did with Earl. So just take your time."

Tammy said, "Yes, Mama I'll do just that."

The next day though, Bob called. It was on a Friday evening. Bob asked Tammy did she want to go out to dinner or something?"

"I don't know. I'm not doing anything, but I don't have a baby sitter. You should have called earlier. I could have got a sitter."

Bob suggested, "Well bring the baby with you. We can go somewhere and sit down to eat with the baby."

Tammy said, "Okay just give me a little time to get myself and the baby ready."

"Call me and I'll be on by."

Tammy and Bob had a good time. Bob was playing with the baby taking up time with her son. Tammy thought that should have been Earl.

"Tammy I really had a nice time," Bob said.

When Tammy got back home she wasn't really thinking too much about Bob, because she was still in love with Earl. She was also hurt from the things Earl had done to her.

Yet, the next few weeks Bob was calling and talking to Tammy periodically. Even Tammy had begun to call Bob to talk with him.

When one weekend came Tammy told Bob she would go out with him. They had a nice time. Everything seemed to be going pretty good. Then Bob started to come by Tammy's house. Within a couple of weeks Tammy made it official with Bob that she would date him. Tammy still had what Mae told her in the back of the mind. Yet she was praying that she had made the right decision and that she did not act too quickly.

"What ever it takes, I'm going to get you over Earl," Bob vowed. "I'll never do the things to you that Earl did to you."

"That's refreshing news," Tammy said. "He really hurt me."

"Yea I understand that. I'll never hurt you like that!"

So they began to spend a lot of time together. Bob called on a regular basis, just to see if she was doing okay, each day. Kay even called because she wanted to know what was going on with Tammy, because she hadn't talked to her in a couple weeks.

"You and Bob are spending a lot of time together. What's up with that Tammy?"

Tammy said, "Yea. I am thinking that maybe he has changed like you said. I didn't think he would stop his old ways. But he seems so much different now."

"Yea I told you he had changed."

Tammy called Fay though to get her point of view.

"You better watch him because I don't know about him. I still don't have no faith in him. You know how he use to lie and go on. This could be one of his lies to 'get you'. You know he always liked you."

"It's too late for those words," Tammy interrupted. "We have already been there girl! And it was alright. He's still calling. He's taking up time with my son and buying him clothes and toys. Bob is also buying me whatever I want and giving me money. I'm going to go on and try him."

Fay said, "Alright Miss Tammy!"

"What do I have to lose?" Tammy asked.

Fay said, "Your heart again and you don't want to do that again?"

"No I was talking to my mom and she was telling me the same thing you're telling me to take my time and go out and have a nice time without any commitments. But I have to admit since Bob and I are dating I don't think about Earl half as much. Plus if we're not going out, Bob is calling."

"Tammy I'm going to say this again, because it seems as if you don't have flash backs. Girl you need to take your time."

The next weekend Bob came by with flowers. He also told Tammy he wanted to take her out shopping. Tammy was so amazed of all of this, because this was something that had never happened to her before. Earl was her 1st love and he never wined and dined her like Bob was doing.

"Well okay Bob we can go out to eat. Mae will keep the baby." Tammy was just having the time of her life.

Months had gone by and Bob came over to visit Tammy. They were sitting on the couch watching a movie. Bob put Tammy in his arms, kissed her, and he got down on one knee and said, "Tammy will you be my wife? And we can make a family."

Tammy was so shocked she was speechless. After Tammy got herself together she said, "Bob I already got a son."

"I'm going to love him like he's my son anyway," he said. "You see we get along, Tammy. So what's the problem?"

Tammy said, "I don't know, just let me

think about it."

"I really love you Tammy."

"Well Bob, I like you a lot too."

"But you will love me though," he emphatically replied.

"I wouldn't doubt that, but I just need a little more time, because you've really been nice to my son and me. I appreciate your kindness very much."

Then a couple months went by. Tammy saw Earl and his wife. They were doing good. Earl didn't even ask Tammy about his son. He just walked by her in the store and acted as if he did not see them. That really pissed Tammy off.

Then the next day Bob called. "I'm still waiting. Let's get married."

"Yea we can get married," Tammy quickly said.

Tammy and Bob were married in March of 1974. It was a very small wedding at their apartment. That should've been a clue to Tammy that those times were going to be difficult, but Tammy was still a clueless teenager. She didn't think. She was just hurt.

Tammy and Bob were married for 6 months when things started to change. They both were working. Tammy was a Certified Nursing Assistant at one of the major hospitals and going to college to meet her goal to be a Registered Nurse. Bob was a delivery boy. He had returned to drinking. Bob later stopped working because of his alcoholism.

"That's okay I'll work some extra shifts and cut back on some of my classes," Tammy told him.

Then Bob got another job the next week. Bob continued to drink real heavily. He lost the job he had just gotten. Bob decided since he was in between jobs he would start selling drugs until he got another job. During that time Bob also started to use drugs and began to go back to his old ways as in high school.

"Why don't you just find a job?" one day Tammy asked.

"I will! Why don't you have a baby for me since I'm taking care of another man's baby?"

Shocked, Tammy snapped back, "No, I'm not ready to have another baby yet, because I want to finish my career. Plus you need a stable job, Bob. We have some bills that need to be paid off; we need to get settled before we even think about having a baby."

Bob got very angry but he went out the next morning and found a job. He even stopped drinking. He wouldn't leave the drugs alone though.

Tammy didn't like the situation so she soon left Bob. Bob didn't hesitate to go by Mae's house where Tammy was. He pleaded to Tammy to please come back home.

"Tammy, I miss you very much," Bob said.

Mae warned her, "Tammy I told you not to marry him. He has relapsed." Tammy really didn't want to hear what Mae was saying. Mae didn't realize she was driving Tammy right back to Bob.

Tammy did go back to Bob. She really wanted to make their marriage work. Things were going good for a while. But Bob changed once more.

"If I were you Tammy," Fay told her, "I'd just leave and never go back."

"Well I want to make my family work," Tammy snapped back. Bob has treated my son and me nicely." At this time Tammy's son was 4 years old.

Yet one day Bob abruptly asked, "I'm not good enough for you to have my child, Tammy?"

Shocked, she calmly and wisely chose her words. "No that's true. I just want to be able to give the children a good life. My first pregnancy was a mistake. I would like for my second one to be planned."

That response still upset Bob. He began an argument. Tammy told Bob that they didn't share the same interest in life, and pointed out that she was finished with that conversation and walked out of the room. Bob stood there with a blank look on his face, but that night Tammy was looking for her birth control pills. She always took them at bedtime. She couldn't find them. She decided to ask Bob had he seen her pills.

"What could I do with your pills Tammy?" he replied but held his head down and couldn't look Tammy in her eyes. Tammy knew then Bob had lied. When Tammy went to bed that night Bob eagerly wanted to have sex. Tammy said "NO" because she had missed taking her pill.

The next morning Tammy called the Doctor to make an appointment. Tammy's appointment had to be week away. Unfortunately, the next night when Tammy went to bed, Bob raped her.

Tammy was now afraid of him and afraid that she might get pregnant. So she decided to sleep on the couch the next night. This infuriated Bob. He dragged her off the couch and into the bed, in spite of Tammy's frantic cries of "NO I'm not getting in bed."

That night nothing happened but Tammy just lay there and thought that this was not the type of man to whom she wanted to be married. He was violently too controlling.

Trying to be the loving wife though, the next day Tammy sat down and had a talk with Bob, after he was calm. She asked him why did he hit her.

"I don't like for you to say no to me," he said.

"I'm human, Bob," she said. "I have feelings too and I don't like to be hit. This marriage isn't going to work with you hitting on me."

Bob went into an apologetic mode. "I'm sorry but I just had too much to drink. I would not hit you again if you just don't leave me."

Tammy thought she should leave but, she decided to stay to make her marriage work.

"Left For Dead"

Tammy left work. She stopped by the grocery store though to pick up a few things for dinner. She was one hour late getting home. Bob was drunk and mad.

"Where in the fuck have you been? You knew I had something to do."

"But you know we needed some food. So I stopped by the store."

"You must have tried to buy the whole damn store," he snorted.

"Whatever," Tammy said. She turned and sat the groceries on the table. Then she started to pour her a glass of soda.

"Bitch you're trying to get smart with me?" Bob grabbed and slapped Tammy so hard she dropped her soda glass.

From the floor, Tammy looked up at Bob. She grabbed the 32-ounce glass soda bottle and hit him in the head. He staggered. Tammy ran to the bedroom and locked the door. Regaining dexterity, Bob started beating on the door.

"Open the door bitch!"

"Leave me alone!" she screamed.
The babies started crying. The oldest one started yelling, "Leave my Mama alone!"

Bob looked at him and left. Tammy came out the bedroom to calm the babies down. She began thinking to herself, "I'm tired of this shit. It's got to stop! We need to talk."

While she was fixing dinner for the children,

Bob did return home with a big bag of marijuana. He went into the kitchen to bag it up. Tammy came in the kitchen.

"Bob, we need to talk!"

"I ain't got time."

"When are you going to have time?"

"I'll let you know." Tammy went back into the bedroom. She turned on the TV and waited for Bob for about an hour.

"What do you want to talk about? You see this lump you put up side my head. I ought to kick your ass."

"Wait a minute," she added. "That's what I want to talk about. I'm tired of all this bull shit, Bob. When we first got married you were working. I don't like you selling drugs around the children, and hitting me. What has gotten into you?"

"I can make more money selling drugs than I can on a white man's job."

"You can't prove that by me. You did good at first. Why don't you get a job? Bob, if you keep this up I'm going to leave you."

"Bitch, if you leave me, I'll kill you. You act like I'm going to be selling drugs all my life."

"Stop calling me a bitch! I'm your wife. Those drugs really have changed you."

"Okay, Tammy you're right. You are my wife." That night everything was okay with Bob and Tammy. They made love to each other this time.

Bob did begin looking for a job. He couldn't find one that he wanted. Two weeks later Bob was back to his old self with all his friends at the house smoking dope. Tammy was very unhappy. Then reality appeared. One evening Tammy was at home. There was a knock on the door. A man stood on the porch. When Tammy opened the door the man asked for Bob.

Her daughter, standing beside her said, "My daddy don't have any nickel bags."

That was the decision-making point for Tammy. She made her mind up to leave Bob.

Tammy was 24-years old with two children. By then she had an eight-year old son and a two-year old daughter. Bob and Tammy still often had arguments because Bob wouldn't work. There was always tension in their house. All he wanted to do was to get something for nothing. He eventually began to sell marijuana out of their house. Tammy wasn't happy with that at all. She was even afraid because she had to leave her children in his care since she worked a swing shift often. This was a very unsafe environment for her children. Her life was becoming very stressful. She often worried.

Tammy still tried to make her marriage work because she didn't want to hear her mother say, "I told you so!" Yet the situation got to the point that Tammy hated to even go home. Lately there was never any love between the two of them. She remembered that she married him on the rebound. Tammy left her ex-husband on May 27, 1979 and moved into an empty apartment, with her two children. She made her desperate move while Bob was sleeping on the couch from over indulging in drinking. All Tammy wanted to do was to get away. Tammy put many clothes in trash bags for that day was her day to do the laundry. Yet, this was a one-time move.

Then she and her children were off to the laundry mat. They all got into the car and left. After Tammy didn't return home the next day. Bob was calling Tammy's job daily asking her to come back to him. At this point Tammy was not ready to reconcile with him. So, on June 7, 1979 Bob came to Tammy's job and threatened her with a knife.

He went ballistic. He kept insisting that she return home with him to make their marriage work. Bob continued to say he didn't know what he was going to do without his daughter. Tammy knew that she had enough of this one-sided relationship. She continued to tell him "no" and that their marriage was over. She insisted and asked him to please leave her job. Bob was removed forcefully by security from the floor. Bob had been drinking that day.

Then Tammy received another call on her job from Bob on June 12,1979. In this call he was calm and requested to see his daughter. He wanted Tammy to meet him at his family's home. Tammy had a gut feeling that something may go wrong, so she was also against the meeting place he suggested.

Tammy suggested that she would meet him at her mother's house at 7:00 P.M. Tammy finished her shift, and began to get very nervous because she knew what she had to deal with as the day came to an end. After Tammy got off work she went to her mother's house where her children were. The children were so excited to see their mother. She too was happy to see them. She still had this strange feeling in her mind, thinking there must be something going to happen even though she knew that she had to face Bob at 7:00 P.M. Tammy's mother had prepared dinner and the table was set. They all sat down for dinner and there was a chilling knock at the door.

Cold chills began running down her spine. When she looked out of the window she saw Bob standing on the porch with his back turned looking out into the street. He was dressed in all black as if he was going to a funeral. When Tammy opened the door, he turned around with a unusual smile on his face.

Bob was also holding a large amount of papers in his hand and a large black and gold stuffed tiger. He gave Tammy the papers that were in his hand. She opened them. They were the foreclosure papers to their house. He tried to explain to her that the house would be taken unless a certain amount of dollars was not paid.

Tammy really didn't care what happened to that drug-trafficking house. She had no intentions of ever returning there. All she wanted from Bob was the keys to her car. Tammy told him that she didn't want any thing else from him. He could have all the furniture and the other car. In return she only wanted her freedom.

Bob smiled and asked Tammy could he take his daughter to the house to see his other son and uncle. She said okay but wanted them to hurry back because she had to go to work the next morning. She also had nursing classes that evening.

Three hours passed before he returned to her mother's house. There was a loud knock on the door. The knock was so hard it awakened Tammy's son who was asleep on the couch, waiting for Bob to return. Tammy went to the door and opened it. She stepped back for him to bring her daughter into the house.

"The baby is asleep in the car. Can you come and get her out of the car so she won't wake up?"

Tammy got to the car. She peculiarly saw the family dog in the back seat. She reached over the dog to remove her daughter from the car.

Before she could do so, Bob pulled her back out of the car door.

"I'm keeping her!" he said. "You need to be coming with me!" They scuffled at the car door. He began cursing and trying to pull Tammy away from the car.

Tammy's mother was in the bathroom rolling her hair and did not hear anything. Tammy's son had been looking out of the screen door.

"Grandmamma, Grandmamma, come and help mommy. Daddy's fighting Mommy. He's going to shoot her." He saw Bob place a 38 caliber pistol under Tammy's chin.

"Bitch, you are coming back home with me," he kept saying while now trying to open the back car door and push in Tammy.

"Why is my life flashing before my eyes?" she thought. By this time her mother came outside to see what was going on, yet before she could make it to her daughter Bob had pulled the trigger. He had shot her under her chin. He then pushed her into his car.

Not knowing that the door was not completely shut and he pulled off at a high rate of speed. The car door came open. He circled the block though and shot at Tammy's mother as she and her grandson ran after the car. They did not see Tammy in the car when it came back. Mae and her grandson continued yelling for help.

"Call 911. Call 911," they kept telling the neighbors. The final bullet missed them. Bob sped away. Others with the grandmother and grandson continued to look for Tammy in the dark.

Suddenly Mae heard crying coming from the corner of the next block, close to the street two blocks away from her house. She called out to her neighbors. "Come quick I founded my baby and my grandbaby in the bushes. Thank you Lord!"

Tammy was unconscious! Yet she held her baby tightly. It was as if she had a death hold on the child. The EMT tried for several minutes to pry her arms open in order to get Tammy to release the baby. They were unable to do it, so Mae asked, "Could I be of some help?"

Mae began to talk to her daughter telling her that everything was going to be all right. That she had to relax and let the baby go. She kept telling Tammy that she loved her very much. Tammy soon released the baby. Mae was so relieved that Tammy responded soon to her. To Mae that was a sign of hope the Lord heard her cry. Mae started to pray to herself, "Lord please save my baby please."

Tammy and her baby too were taken to the City Hospital. Tammy was still unconscious. She was placed on life support while she was in the ambulance in route to the hospital. When Tammy got to the hospital she was taken right to surgery. While Tammy was in surgery Mae called her own best friend Katie. Mae was so shaken but she needed to tell her what had just happened to her child.

Katie answered the telephone and Mae let out a loud yell. Tears rolled down her cheeks.

"Miss Mae, what's wrong? Why are you so hysterical?"

"That bastard shot my baby. He shot my baby! I'm at the City Hospital right now. Five times. Tammy was shot five times!"

"I'll be there as soon as I can." Once Katie got to the hospital and was able to calm Mae down she asked her to call Tammy's best friends Fay and

Kay. Tammy's friends made it to the hospital in disbelief.

Fay scolded Kay. "I told you that he was no good but you wanted to believe that he had changed. The only things he had changed were his clothes."

"I'm just so sorry," Kay said. "I never thought this would happen. God please help Tammy."

"We're very concerned about the gun shot to the head," the surgeon told the family. "That was the one that had done the most damage. The bullet entered the cerebellum."

They said that was the structure of the brain regulation of complex voluntary muscular movement. The doctor was unable to remove all the pellets from the brain so they only removed the ones that they could. Tammy remained in ICU for four weeks and during those four weeks she also remained unconscious.

The Dream

Then God started to work with Tammy through her unconscious mind and dreams. The first most powerful dream Tammy had was that she was being shocked with a wool blanket. This was God's way of awaking his child. There was sharp stimulation to the body all over. The nerves of the body came alive.

There was another dream that had a very powerful effect. This dream was about a white flexible straw. Tammy was told by a very meek voice to get on the straw, in the water and ski across the body of water. The water was such a pretty sky-blue at this time. She was standing on land.

The straw appeared at her feet. The meek voice said "Get on the straw now and ski across the body of water. If you're able to balance your body there will be a new life for you on the other side."

Tammy did as the voice instructed her to do. She was floating on a straw going across this large body of water. On the other side there was a different feeling. There was a feeling of security. Tammy had received a great gift from following the instructions of the meek voice.

Within several days Tammy regained consciousness. She was able to open her eyes and focus. Tammy was able to recognize her mother and friends. She wasn't able to move her left side. She was semi-paralyzed. Tammy was unable to eat too. She was being nourished with a feeding tube in her nose. Tammy's jaw was wired together. She had sustained a broken jaw from the bullet that went through her chin.

The Doctors at the hospital finally upgraded Tammy's condition from critical to stable. After Tammy regained consciousness her Doctor explained her condition to her. All she could think about were the bullets. Tammy was afraid of just one bullet and to know that she came in contact with five bullets at one time, was a bit much. She began to thank God, the only man who loved her.

Tammy was very excited to know that her condition had been upgraded. By getting that information she knew that she would be moved out of ICU and into her own room. Now her children were able to visit. The first visit Tammy had with her children had to be in the waiting room, because the children were under-age. Tammy didn't realize that, because her heart was so set on seeing her children.

One of the nurses put Tammy in a Geri-chair and rolled her to the waiting room. Tammy was too weak to sit up in a wheel chair at that time. When she saw her children, her mother, and her grandfather she smiled. Her eight-year-old son put his head down and began to cry.

Tammy asked him what was wrong he said to Tammy "Why Mama did he do this to you?"

"Honey I don't know? But we should pray that God heals my body each night before we go to bed."

"Mama, I'll pray every night."

Tammy embraced him the best that she could, and gave him a big kiss. By that time Tammy's 3-year-old daughter Nicole was trying to climb into her mother's lap. Tammy's mother had to pull her down and explain that her mother was too weak to hold her now. One of the nurses asked Nicole did she know what happened to her mother?

Nicole replied "My daddy shot my Mama a lots of times and I hate him."

The nurse replied, "See you do know what happened. You're a smart girl."

Tammy still had to do some hard work before her life would ever become normal again. She was moved, from the City hospital to a private hospital to start physical therapy. The private hospital was the hospital where Tammy was working.

She had been employed there for five years. The miracle of this move was that Tammy was actually moved to a floor where she had worked, so all the staff on that floor knew her and God put her on the floor. She knew that she would receive the best of care.

On the first day of therapy Tammy found out that she had no muscle control. She was sitting in a wheelchair unable to hold her head up. She didn't know that her left arm was hanging out of the wheel chair until the nurse asked her to try to hold it up. At this point Tammy had to take notice of where her limbs were.

When she arrived in therapy, the first thing the therapist did was to put Tammy's body on a large beach ball and bounce it up and down. This was an exercise to strengthen the muscles and to get them back into shape. Tammy's muscles had died.

During therapy session she had to work very hard. She wanted to get well enough to take care of her children. Tammy had to learn how to walk. Her whole body was shaking. She couldn't stand alone. There were times when it got so tough she didn't know what to do. Tammy kept on praying to God for strength and to be able to rear her children.

Therapy continued. She had to learn how to dress. Just putting on a bra was a very hard task for Tammy to do. Her fingers weren't coordinated. She had to learn how to use her hands. She couldn't even fasten her own blouse.

Occupational therapy taught her how to do her daily living as dressing herself. Sometimes things got a little hard. She had to ask the Lord for strength. Her hands would shake as she attempted to do things. Tammy had to teach herself how to read and write again. She still wasn't able to walk. Tammy knew that before she could go home she had to be able to walk. God kept working with Tammy through her dreams. She continued to have the dream about the white straw. Tammy began to stand as she held the walking bars in therapy; she was able to hold onto the bars and make baby steps.

Sometimes Tammy would fall back. Her muscles in her buttock had to be strengthened therefore her muscles were being trained to be normal. Just being a normal person meant that she could just get up out of a chair and walk, not realizing the need for buttock muscles to walk.

Tammy was going through a great deal of changes thinking she would never walk. She was semi-paralyzed. She had to work harder. She had to pray harder. As time went on the feeding tube was removed and Tammy was able to eat soft food, but her jaws remained wired. Tammy was happy about when she was ready to eat pureed food. But the nurses had to put milk in the food so that Tammy could drink it through a straw.

Oh that white flexible straw played a big roll in Tammy's life. Tammy had a gap between her teeth so she was able to drink her meals through her teeth with that white straw. Tammy thought to herself that, that was a big improvement. Then she began to feed herself yet still unable to use her left hand.

Tammy thought to herself that it was a blessing that she was right-handed. Several months went by and Tammy continued to work hard in therapy. She wanted to be with her mother and two children. Her life wouldn't be complete without her family.

She prayed every night for God to strengthen her body and mind so that she could get up out of that hospital bed and go home to her mother. Tammy would work on the exercises that therapy was doing while she was in bed also while she was sitting in her wheel chair. Tammy would continue to tighten her buttock muscles up while she was sitting or lying on them. She would also use a tennis ball in her left hand to strengthen her hand. She knew that one day God was going to answer her prayers. She knew all she needed was as the scripture said, to have as much "Faith as a grain of a mustard seed and nothing shall be impossible unto you," (Matthew 17:20).

Tammy continued to pray and to be positive knowing that one day God was going to answer her. One day in therapy she graduated from the bars to a walker without wheels. Tammy was so happy she was able to get up alone out of a wheel chair. One never knows what great feeling that is until being there.

One day Tammy was able to put on her own bra. Each day her body was changing. Therapy and occupational therapy were working with her, but at this point it was time for the healing process and God was the only one. Only God could control this.

Human minds could do only so much, the rest was up to God.

Days went by. Tammy started to walk with a four prone cane. Life was looking a lot brighter. Then on August 28, 1979, Tammy's Doctor came in her room and discharged her. Tammy was so excited she called her mother to tell her Mother she could come and pick up her.

When Tammy's mother got to the hospital to get her daughter, she had Tammy's children in the car. Tammy still had a great deal of work to do. Her work was for her to regain her self-esteem. It had been knocked all the way down. The only way she could do that was to put God first in everything that she did, and to stay positive.

Tammy's friends came over when she got home to visit. Tammy's mother had to have some help with Tammy's care. There were still a lot of tasks that Tammy was unable to do. Tammy would need someone to stay with her while her mother worked. Tammy's friends Fay and Kay took turns when they could, also a few family members helped.

After Tammy had been home for a week or two, Bob called and wanted to see his daughter. Tammy slammed down the telephone. He was not even in jail! Did the police even arrest him? Society had taught him that he could "get away with murder". A murderer was still free. Society had refused to protect Tammy.

So she had to develop courage. They really didn't have any thing to discuss. Tammy thought to herself that Bob really lost his mind. She had almost lost her life once and by the grace of God she was still alive. Bob would never get another chance to repeat what he had done. Tammy became afraid to live in the same city though. Tammy was unable to sleep at night. Then she called her father who lived in St. Louis and asked him to come and get her. Tammy's father came to get her and her children the next weekend. Tammy moved to St. Louis, Missouri. She moved with her father, and his family. Tammy was now able to walk with a normal cane. She still would be off balance at times. Her left side was still numb. It felt heavy, but Tammy could move it. There was a lot of work to be done, but it was no longer physical work; it was spiritual and mental.

Unfortunately, being in a human mind set, all Tammy could think about was how she was going to support her children. The questions in her mind were could she get a job? Who would hire her with a dismantled body? The only skills she had were in healthcare and sales. On the other hand when Tammy looked in the mirror at herself, the self-esteem she once had was in question. Tammy mind wondered back to her dream she had when she was balancing herself on a white flexible straw across a large body of water. In reality that body of blue water was Tammy's new life. It was the life that The Almighty God had given to her. After Tammy was able to relate to God in body and soul, her questions were answered through the works of God. When Tammy moved to St. Louis it was a whole different world. There she had no friends. But Tammy realized that there was one friend with her always. She knew that He would be with her at all times. She could call any time and His line was never busy.

Tammy began to attend church very often. The pastor of the local church was a female; a very different female. She was a person that was filled with God's love. When anyone was close to her anyone could feel her power. She took Tammy under her wings; it was like a transformation.

Tammy's self-esteem was damaged. Her whole life was upside down. She needed a lift in spirit because she began to look at her condition physically and mentally. There was nothing she could do. She went back to her up-bringing. She thought about the things her grandparents had gone through. They never gave up and they stayed on course with God. She watched her mother doing the same thing that her parents did. She was only making $25.00 a week ($100.00 a month) and had one child to take care of and she made it. Looking back on her family life gave her the incentive to run on to see what the end was going to be. Tammy knew that she needed something that was bigger than she. Tammy needed The Holy Ghost. The Holy Ghost was something that could help her to overcome her problems no matter how big or small.

Tammy tarried for the Holy Ghost on a Thursday night in January of 1980. (She knew that Tarrying was to stay for a time to wait.) The service was very high in Spirit. The Pastor's face was glowing; the members prayed and waited on the Lord; all the saints were on one accord. The chanting and the tambourines were so powerful.

New Life, New Love, New Savior

After the high praising service she was filled
with the Holy Spirit. She felt new even though she
still had a dismembered body. She knew that the
Lord was going to work things out for her. She had
been renewed in the Sprit of her mind according to
Ephesians 4:23.

She didn't feel as she did before. She felt
uplifted. Her soul was rejoicing. Tammy was
thinking to herself while she was sitting on the
Church bench that she could do anything with the
Lord on her side. All the pity she had been feeling
for herself had just vanished. She was walking a
new walk and talking a new talk in God's name.
Her pastor would see her sometimes just looking off
with a blank expression. She would anoint her head
with blessed oil and tell her everything was going to
be okay. Tammy said "She doesn't have anything."

In reply the Pastor said "You will be
blessed." Tammy just looked at her and smiled.

Tammy began to rebuild her life but it was
being rebuilt through God not by her. The Pastor
would pray for the healing of her body. Over a
period of time Tammy was able to walk without a
cane. She was walking well, but was limping just a
little. Tammy was now able to move around. She
was able to drive a car. Tammy began to look for a
job. She didn't want to live on Government funds.

Tammy's aunt was working at a local hospital.
She hadn't seen Tammy since she was a baby. She
told Tammy's father that she might be able to help

Tammy get a job in her field. Tammy's father drove her to the hospital on what you would call a dry run. There was one problem. It was at night and he went through a park that had many exits. When it was her turn to drive alone, Tammy took the wrong exit and it seemed as if she was in a maze. There were so many large trees.

Finally she saw a street that went to a service station. The service station attendant was able to give her the correct directions to the hospital. Tammy had prayed that night before she made her trip to the hospital to put in the application. She asked God to give her what she needed to live her life with and to guide her. Tammy knew that God would work it out. With God's grace Tammy knew that she would get the job.

Tammy put God in front of her when she went into the human service office. There was a man sitting at the desk. He asked Tammy "May I help you?"

Tammy told him she was there to fill out an application. The man gave her the application. Tammy had another problem that she asked God to help her with; she wasn't able to write well. Through the whole application process it was a trying thing. It seemed as if God took that ink pen and filled out that application. When God and Tammy completed the application she handed it to the man.

He said, "Thank you. We'll call you if we get an opening."

As Tammy walked out of the office she could feel the eyes on her, but she kept her focus on God, and knew to not to worry about people. When Tammy left that building she left everything in

God's hand. Tammy was very excited because she knew that she had the job. She had already claimed it.

Tammy found her way back home without any problems. She had met a friend named Lee and he showed her a different way to her job. Tammy met Lee one night when she, her father and his wife were going to church in the month of September. They had to stop to pick up his mother-in-law. When Tammy went into the house she saw this handsome man lying on the couch. This was her stepmother's brother. He looked at Tammy and said hello and smiled. In return Tammy said hello and smiled. Tammy thought to herself "what a feeling".

Lee dropped by his sister's house one evening and Tammy and he began to talk about her job. She was excited about talking to him. Then Lee asked her what route was she taking to get to the job. Tammy told him the route that she was taking, and Lee explained to her that he knew a better route. He would come to show her a better way to get to the job.

One week later Tammy received a telephone call from the hospital. They were asking her to come in the next morning for an interview at 8 A.M. Tammy was so excited. She called Lee right away to tell him so he could share her excitement. Tammy called her mother to give her the good news. She gave her father & step-mother the good news when they got home from work. It felt so good to Tammy to have good news to share. To her it was God working his miracles in spite of what had happened.

Tammy knew through determination and with the strength of the Lord she could stand for God in difficult and challenging situations. "When we do that, God will vindicate us and will ultimately take the glory," she thought.

On October 1979, Lee came by his sister's house to see if he could help Tammy. He took Tammy for a ride to show her around St. Louis and also to show her a different route to the hospital. During the ride Lee asked Tammy if she was hungry.

"Yes, what type of food did you have in mind?" she asked.

"How about a rib tip? I know this place that serves good rib-tip sandwiches and it is close by."

"I've never had a rib-tip on a sandwich but I will try it," she replied. When they got to the restaurant she was happy that it was a carry out restaurant. Tammy remained in the car just watching all the people going in and out. About 15 minutes, Lee came out with a large brown bag.

Lee asked Tammy if she was going to eat her sandwich. Tammy was somewhat shy. It had really been a long time since she had a man to buy her dinner and she was too nervous to eat in front of him. Tammy didn't want to waste any sauce on her. She said that she would be very embarrassed if that happened.

Tammy was going through her teenage stage again at 24 years old. She really liked Lee. She wanted to make a good impression on him. Lee joked with Tammy and told her if she didn't eat her sandwich he would. They both laughed.

Lee took Tammy down a long street with lots of stop signs on it. Then he showed her the hospital where she would be working. They took the same route back. Tammy told Lee that was a better way than her father had taken her. It was almost a straight shot.

Lee brought Tammy back home. He went in and talked with his sister and Tammy's father. Tammy also introduced him to her children. The children were somewhat shy. They just said, "Hello" to Lee. Then they continued to watch TV. Lee left. Later he and Tammy began to call each other often. Lee told Tammy that he had other women, but he wasn't happy with their relationship. Yet Lee told Tammy that he had to put her on his schedule for another date.

Tammy felt that would never work out, because of what had happen in her life. She thought no man would ever date her and feel comfortable. Yet, Lee was a very special man. He wasn't looking at the outside of Tammy, he was looking at the inside. He saw the compassion in her heart. He also saw her children among other qualities she had.

Tammy asked Lee if he pitied her.

Lee stated, "If I pity you there couldn't be a relationship."

Tammy never wanted pity because she was so independent. That frame of mind started when she was 6 years – old when her grand father gave her a hoe to chop cotton. He taught her independence and to always work for what she wanted.

Tammy was now in competition with the other women. Lee had been in a relationship with each of these women. Tammy really cared for Lee. He was a different kind of man. Lee had a little bad boy in him with charm.

Lee saw something else in Tammy too that he didn't see in the other women. Tammy was very intelligent, neat, and a hard worker. Tammy wanted things in life and Lee thought she would make a good wife. But Lee wanted to put Tammy on hold (or you may say in the Layaway until he was ready.) Even though Lee wasn't ready for a wife, Lee couldn't let Tammy get away.

The things that Lee was into he couldn't let go right away, because Lee was a "Lady's Man". After a while when Lee thought the time was right he asked Tammy to marry him. Even though Tammy's life had its hardship she had to move on with her life and let God work it out.

Tammy said, "Yes!" to Lee's proposal. The children were happy for their mother and Lee. But Tammy's son was very protective of his mother. He remembered what had happened in her last relationship with Bob. Tammy's daughter liked Lee very much though.

After they got married some of Lee's past came to haunt him. The women began to call him and come to his job. By this time, Lee and Tammy were going to church each Sunday. The women began to come to church. This upset Tammy.

"I can't even serve God without the women arguing in church with Lee. Lee told Tammy to just give him a little time to clear the situation.

Tammy called her daddy and asked him to take her back home to Memphis. Even though she was afraid to go home, she just didn't have anywhere else to go. Tammy left Lee, but she didn't want to hear her dad say "I told you so."

Lee told Tammy that he would come to visit her and he would send her some money for the children. Lee told Tammy that he loved her and Tammy told Lee she loved him too. This made Tammy feel good because she thought she couldn't compete with the other women. Lee told Tammy when school was out he would come and take her back to St. Louis. Lee came and got Tammy within a year. After Tammy and Lee got back together his job shut down. Lee told Tammy to just stay with him and he would make every thing alright. Tammy told Lee that she'd never leave him.

Unfortunately, Lee went back to some of his old habits. Tammy didn't like that at all. Yet, Lee was trying to make some money. Lee told Tammy he would stop as soon as he found a job. Tammy reminded Lee that she was working.

Lee said "That's not enough. I don't want you to take care of me, I'm the man I should be the one to take care of my family."

Tammy told Lee that she understood, but Tammy would make a mental note of how long he would be away from home each day. Tammy was unhappy because she saw how stressed out he was, and he needed her help, even though he would come home with some money with no explanation. Lee felt like he didn't need an explanation, but Tammy did. Lee told Tammy everything was going to be okay, because he truly loved her.

Tammy decided that she was going to help Lee find a job after she saw what it was doing to him each day. Tammy began to send out resumes for jobs from newspaper ads. Tammy asked around to see if any body knew any place that was hiring. Eventually, Lee not only got one job but he ended up with two. Lee decided to stop Tammy from working and sent her back to school. Tammy didn't think she could function well enough in school because of what she had been through, but Lee encouraged her.

Tammy prayed and went back to school. Lee did what he said he would. He studied with her, and Tammy graduated as a Registered Nurse. Tammy told Lee that he should then quit one of the jobs.

Lee was a supervisor on one of his jobs. The company transferred him to Florida to help them set up a new job. Lee left Tammy home and she planned to join him in 3 months, after he had gotten settled. Lee and Tammy talked with each other nightly. Tammy was missing Lee day by day. The children had grown up to begin their own lives. Tammy thought to herself it would be nice to do some traveling. So Tammy would often take trips to Mississippi to visit her mother on special occasions.

Then years had gone by. Tammy's mother got sick. Lee didn't want to leave his job after 18 years. But after he saw how worried Tammy was he left his job, because he truly loved Tammy. They moved so Tammy could take care of her mother. Tammy's mother got better and moved in with Tammy and Lee. Tammy was very happy to have her mother with them. Tammy missed her for twenty years.

God made everything possible. Lee got a job at a company as a supervisor. Tammy got a job at a local hospital. Tammy and Lee began to go to church each Sunday. Lee soon became a Deacon of the church and the Sunday school superintendent. Tammy was very proud of her husband.

Later God called Lee to preach. Lee and Tammy realized it was God's plan all the time.

The moral of the story is to all women. "If you are in an abusive relationship you should put your faith in God and he'll take care of your situation."